THE LIBRARY
ST. MARY'S COLLEGE OF MARYLAND
ST. MARY'S CITY, MARYLAND 20686

D1557325

Fishing
For
Myth

Fishing for Myth

Poems by

Heid E. Erdrich

Minnesota Voices Project Number 79

NEW RIVERS PRESS 1997

Copyright ©1997 by Heid Ellen Erdrich
Library of Congress Catalog Card Number 97-65062
ISBN 0-89823-174-4
All rights reserved
Edited by Leslie Adrienne Miller
Copy edited by Jim Cihlar
Proofread by Julie Thomson
Typesetting and book design by Barb Patrie Design
Cover illustration by Angie Erdrich

New Rivers Press is a non-profit literary press dedicated to publishing
the very best emerging writers in our region, nation, and world.

The publication of Fishing for Myth has been made possible by
generous grants from the Jerome Foundation; the North Dakota
Council on the Arts; the South Dakota Arts Council; Target Stores,
Dayton's, and Mervyn's by the Dayton Hudson Foundation; and the
James R. Thorpe Foundation.

Additional support has been provided by the Elmer L. and
Eleanor J. Andersen Foundation, the Beim Foundation, General Mills
Foundation, Liberty State Bank, the McKnight Foundation, the Star
Tribune/Cowles Media Company, the Tennant Company Foundation,
and the contributing members of New Rivers Press. New Rivers is a
member agency of United Arts.

UNITED ARTS·   NORTH DAKOTA COUNCIL   SOUTH DAKOTA ARTS COUNCIL
                        FOR THE ARTS

Fishing for Myth has been manufactured in Canada for New Rivers
Press, 420 North 5th Street, Suite 910, Minneapolis, MN 55401.
First Edition.

To JEB
who removes all snags from the river,
takes my lure, and keeps me in line.

Acknowledgments

Fishing for Myth owes a great deal of its final shape to Leslie Adrienne Miller, poet and patient editor. Thanks also to C.W. Truesdale and everyone at New Rivers Press, to the Inroads Native American Program at The Loft, the Native Art Circle Writers, the Johns Hopkins Writing Seminars, Cleopatra Mathis, Cheryl Two Bears, Jonis Agee, Susan Welch, Pauline Brunette Danforth, and especially to my muse of food, Helen Miller. Every day I'm grateful to my imaginative parents and understanding family, especially to my sisters Angie and Louise who make pictures, and Lise who takes me places. My ultimate and humble thanks go to John Burke—husband who makes all things possible.

Grateful acknowledgment goes to the editors of the following publications in which some of these poems appeared, sometimes in earlier versions: *Tamaqua, City Paper, Hurricane Alice, Maryland Poetry Review, Raven Chronicles, Great River Review, Cimarron Review, Prairie Volcano, The Party Train, Stones for the Fire, The Colour of Resistance.*

Julia Badger quote on page 37 is from *Wisconsin Chippewa Myths & Tales*, Victor Barnouw.

Table of Contents

III SYSTEMS OF DIVINATION

If myths are impossibilities, they are to be believed with fervor in no small part due to their quality of impossibility.

CHRISTOPHER VESCHY, **Imagine Ourselves Richly**

I

Origin Stories

True Myth

Tell a child she is composed of parts
(her Ojibway quarters, her German half-heart)
she'll find the existence of harpies easy
to swallow. Storybook children never come close
to her mix, but manticores make great uncles,
Sphinx a cousin she'll allow, centaurs better to love
than boys—the horse part, at least, she can ride.
With a bestiary for a family album she's proud.
Her heap of blankets, her garbage grin, prove
she's descended of bears, her totem, it's true.
And that German witch with the candy roof,
that was her ancestor too. If swans can rain
white rape from heaven, then what is a girl to do?
Believe her Indian eyes, her sly French smile,
her breast with its veins skim milk blue—
She is the myth that is true.

Origin of Poem

Your storyself might rise
to a canoeing woman,
her soft-leather face,
black eyebrow swoops,
swallows skimming
a brown lake.

She could sing,
hushkee hush darling,
suu suu lah-lee
speak only to me.

Listen to her.
See how she bears it,
fins air for us.

She could ripple water,
surface like a fish,
gulp this world down whole.

In a pool,
in your own cupped hands
a carp rises.
One moment of recognition
then waters to nowhere
just lap lap lap.

We fish our own waters
green and layered
weedy and warm—
Nothing rises,
no ripples, but we wait.
All we want is the tug—
something deep, alive, on the line.

Creation

I

That March we were thirteen,
best friends dressed as twins, in love
the way young girls love mirrors,
anything to better see ourselves.
But any lingering look from any male
broke us open fiercely, too early
like the dandelions we tore—green buds
opening to the yellow, unformed flowers.

II

In the heat beaten late July garden
of the Lutheran Home for Girls, the arc
of her pregnancy strains to the sun.
Thick air drapes about her, she wears it.
A neat garden rolls out for her. A path
beside a birdbath ends in knee-deep columbine.
I imagine Eve there, Eve who likes gardens.
She pinches the flowers' honey–filled tips,
brushes past sunflowers who spend their whole
enraptured day bending, like lovers, for the light—
She shakes pollen from the seed heads, claps
her hands, watches yellow clouds rise up, disperse.
Then Eve sings, holding out notes long
and clear as love. But my friend hears
only the noise of the garden—
the vibration of pistil and stamen,
the loud love-making petals,
every plant humming for release.

Boyfriend

He was ugly as a troll and sturdy as a troll. His stubby arms and legs bunched with muscles, his chest was barrel-wide and hairless. His grin half looped up his cheeks like a happy face. Though not a simpleton, he smiled most of the time. And yet no woman would have him.

When called Pumpkin Head or Pie Face, he stamped with fury, growled like the Tasmanian Devil and turned the deadly ray of his piggly gray eyes upon the name-caller. He shut whole restaurants up. Men twice his size wouldn't mess with him. And yet no woman would have him.

With his father always curled on their couch like a pickled fetus, and his mom with her pug-dog face, with her punched-in face of a drunk's wife—what did he have to be beautiful for?

Greasy to his elbows, monkey in a car engine, handy with tools—you wouldn't want him with your daughter, but let him slide beneath your junk cars, slide into that dark and private world of parts—He charmed cars, or cursed them with his boot tips, screaming, *Work you dog fucker! Dog fucker! I'll kick you to death, you dog!*

No woman would love him, but I did. I was a girl. Think of how beautiful we all were once and how we learned to love the beast.

Sweeping Heaven

Someone has to sweep these million golden
steps to God's throne, but not for long.
Not since I swept aside some lapis clouds
and glimpsed in the swirl what shone
through heaven's great vaulted window—
the whirling, light-studded universe below.
All the years I've swept his throne, God never
said a word. Now this broom weighs
in my hands like stone. I hurl it down,
watch it shoot sparks of shattered glass
into the slow deep. My wings grow fiery,
sear me to their roots. Cold heaven cannot keep
such a molten soul—I cast myself out to plummet
on useless wings. My hair a flaming comet, I burn
through countless atmospheres. Hurtling, contracting,
cooling to a blue-white, gem-hard point, I strike a hole
in the starry roof of a North Dakota night, and sink
through a girl's unblinking eye, and settle below her throat.
There I stretch, though my wings won't rest. They beat
hard in her chest until she feels swept through inside
by something restless, something opening so wide
it showers like the wheeling prairie sky.

Breaking and Entering

She kept a stash of forbidden matches,
got caught dropping splashes of wax on her bed.
Iced-over sidewalks, the ones I loved to skim,
she cracked with her hard heel. All I got was
water welling up where she walked. Still, I followed
through the shards, saw her jump in some boy's car.
She started the dream—a storm with flat hands
bangs on all the windows, a storm in a green gown
with rain-dark hair. This girl, who wouldn't lift
her gray eyes to her mother's gaze, would make love
in old farmhouses, on abandoned boxsprings,
on scoured linoleum, in rusted bathtubs,
junked trucks along windbreaks.
She broke in, she told me, not to love
those boys, but to melt them down,
look them in the eye and crack their glaze.
She started the dream—a storm pries the edge
off the roof, lifts my lids, glares at me with a gray eye
that strikes on love, that can get past all human walls.

The Red River of the North

Like all water it cares for its creatures.
They draw each drop they drink from it,
and when they paw the ground or cut
a furrow in a field, river scent comes up.
They trust its unusual course, the path
lapping flat as a tongue to Canada.
In their veins there's a pull
direct as that flow: North,
forever, even through winter
frozen four-feet thick or breaking
in spring, surging ice chunks big as cars—
it brims in ditches, on roads, when it seeps
into fields, leaves June sloughs thick with cattails
that brown and explode as the dry July wind
whips fields into thirty-foot spires of dust.
Drought drives the river underground,
exposes its bed: bottles and jars,
stranded fish sloughing their flesh,
washboards and tires,
the river's bone and core.
People pick about for souvenirs.
Though the bullhead's flesh tastes muddy,
boys pull squirming netfuls from puddles.
And the snapping turtles, all plates and claws,
some big enough for a child to stand on,
their hundred-year-old faces
sunk in rings of wrinkles,
bask peacefully on strands between ponds,
while beside the bridge abutment
young drunks park in their pickups.
They have come for the snappers,
easy catches in a river so low.
They break branches, lurch toward
the turtles whose jaws lock,
clench the sticks, hold

and hold even as they are lifted,
even at the shock of the hatchet.
Shell trunks trudge headless,
straight toward the water.
The young men laugh long laughs
throwing their own heads back.
They do not notice the sky go green,
hung with hail teats to the west.
Herons, blue as smoke, rise,
seek higher ground. In the muck,
the men gather turtles, toss the bodies
in the truckbed where reflex
makes the reptile's nails kick
a scratching call the river answers
in a flash of rain. The trickle swells,
sucks ankle deep, whorls to the men's lips,
pours and rushes into them, washes them
until they drink a first watery breath
in a world of heron and catfish—
This is the river ignorant of banks
and dikes and bridges, swimming back,
wanting only to rise and rise beyond
what binding or straightening inflicts,
wanting to fill its creatures
with insistent murkiness, the cold urge
that pumps in every pulse: North
the way our blood goes in its sleep,
the way all things must go
in shells or scales or feathers.

Oxbow

TO ASIGANAK

Go to one of those little islands on the prairie
that haven't been broken and stitched with wheat—
Where the river has swung a loop
out of its ancient path—
Where mounds of earth along the slough
form sculptures only the sky can see—
Watch meadowlarks thrust
their banded throats up and warble
their yellow heads off—
Listen as yellow-headed blackbirds,
bobbing on reeds, ricochet their untuned calls—
Taste juneberry, chokecherry, wild plum—
See how the redwing blackbirds took
their showy epaulettes
from the high-bush cranberries—
Hear how that tart fruit
cracked their voices for good.

One Girl

These were decent people,
publishing the salaries of public employees,
their indiscretions and local tragedies.
They came from a land of hunger
to this place protected from storms
according to an old Indian blessing.
It seemed everyone made way:
the old ones who called the land holy;
even the ancient lake drew back her flat
skirt of waters leaving good black earth.
They built up the lowlands, drained ponds,
pushed back the river banks to plant grain.
They made this place rise like bread.

One Girl walked right out of the earth.
She stood on their bridge telling their sons
the story of the river in its own language.
Those boys returned home silent or,
against their mother's glances, tried words
that broke and stumbled like water over rocks.
One Girl stood during storms on their bridge,
watching funnels draw up into clouds passing close,
as though she had come to take that leftover blessing,
let the tornado slam like a freight train down main street.

They drove her out of town through their graveyard,
through stubbled wheat by the watertower.
And then did they see? Her heart cracked open,
a sack of hard yellow feed, spilled for crows to pick.
The black wind wrapped her body.
Her tattered cries flapped away like birds.
Now, to boys who would speak it,
even her name sounds far away.

Rich Hour

GULF WAR, 1991

Starlings, those blue-black and shaggy birds whose feathers seem secondhand, starlings I've never liked. But for now, because the warring world beyond this courtyard has gone grey, lit with silent twisting flashes, for now I am happy they stay.

True, starlings kill tree tops, drop their messes lavishly, even where they eat. Still, they're social birds, seldom alone, always regarding one another with quick birdy glances, always whistling "whew" as in "that was a close one"—to which I always whisper, "yes, it was."

Perhaps I'm deluded, only imagining this blue rectangle of sky is the last door anywhere left open to the sun. Why else would the birds flock here?

A mockingbird rushes the starlings. To spite them she opens the fountain of her throat and the sweetest sounds known to birds come out: the all-clear signal, the *love here* signal, the universal call to drink the dew before the day does.

I am not distracted. I've only grown full with war and these milling starlings, these indifferent streetfolk bored by the mockingbird's lulling, evening voice.

Now I see, war works like grief—makes vision sharp, more rare, so it is clear I have always been here, in this courtyard, with these starlings scrabbling at my feet, with the mockingbird's words printed on air, the blue door closing above me.

Human Map

ALL QUOTES FROM: "BY ANALYZING DNA SAMPLES FROM 400 ETHNIC
GROUPS, SCIENTISTS COULD RECONSTRUCT HUMAN HISTORY,"
BOYCE RENSBERGER, *WASHINGTON POST*, MARCH 15-21, 1993

You will be happy to know someone has asked our cells to tell,
in their own bloody language, whether or not all Indian tribes
descend from a single group that migrated from Asia.

Your own body contains the answer and the map: "Hidden within
the DNA of each human being is a record of that person's ethnic history."
Just one drop can read like a mystery.

All the way back to "humanity's dim evolutionary past,"
without a flashlight, scientists can trace
"the ancient migrations and ancestral intermixings
that have shaped every tribe and culture on Earth."

Still, it's too late to test Sky Woman, whose breath of life exists
in all creatures, or Thought Woman, who imagines us even now,
or any of the First Beings who survived by tricks.

Too late, so they will have to settle for *your* blood.

Some tribal jokesters call this *The Vampire Project*. Rumor has it
donations need no consent and any clinic might be in on it—so
go ahead—Give Blood! It's your civic duty.

Anthropologists, our old friends, support this "needy and urgent
cause." And who knows? You may be one of the "HIP people"
(Historically Interesting Population)
who, they note, are vanishing at an alarming rate.

Vanishing? They make it sound so passive, as if whole peoples
simply fade away.

You say you won't go to the blood drive? But the needle's nothing new. Bloodshed always determines who inherits a patch of earth. Even they admit their findings might be used to support "increasingly incendiary claims of land tenure in ethnic disputes."

Do not fear this genetic tattooing—if they keep it up long enough, they will discover we all belong to one mother.

Scholars insist "the concept of race long ago lost its scientific validity." And you know how well the general public embraces these subtle distinctions and complex genetic notions.
Soon racism *as we know it* will end.

Whether we help them or not is no matter. Our blood will out.
Our bodies' code will crack. They will have their map.

Worlds from Water

Always,
Loon, her red eye a dart in darkness,
pulls for the earth in a mouthful
of pond bottom and duckgrass—
Always,
Turtle, her neck strained to point
with hook-hard nose,
heaves plate-tectonic shoulders,
so borders are waters,
the world served on halfshells—
Always,
Water, drifted with tobacco,
waves and parts before Person,
vessel of water carried on water,
until, bound out of that same blue,
what in 1492 was found
was also lost—

Fourth of July Electrical Storm

I

I take you on a family picnic
by a dam so slow it stinks.
Pelicans feed on the stunned
trash fish churning belly-up
below the concrete ducts.
Strange birds like dinosaurs,
odd bones notched on impossibly
long beaks—not beaks,
more like ivory-hinged satchels
or elegant trashcan lids.

We drive to White Rock Colony,
fallen town on the border. Trees,
twisted into fretful shapes and gray
as the abandoned houses, fill
with loud birds out of territory:
Red Shafted Flickers, Thrashers,
one Great Crested Flycatcher.

II

Why have I brought you with us?
First to the smelly dam
which does not yet signify,
then to a ghost town where we saw
no ghosts except the sculpted rebar outline
of the white rock blasted out to make room
for a grain elevator that's gone too,
only a hundred years since they drove
the Dakota from this land.

Maybe this is why I have you along:
We had been to the pow-wow at Sisseton.
The arbor of dried leaves couldn't cut the heat.
Tired dancers sweated out in the arena.
Kids fooling in the dust behind the bleachers
grew fussy and loud with thirst.

Did I tell you we had the boys with?
Their new haircuts buzzed short as the velvet
on antlers. We had come over the border
for fireworks. That's a hopeful image, isn't it?
American boys blasting Blackcats and Whistlers,
furls of spangled paper in the ditches.

III

Heading back north, we see a gray funnel
fingering the clouds over Wahpeton.
We best get home, my father cautions.
And I say, Home? But Dad, *the tornado is there!*

You must wonder how he convinces us to drive
into that darkness. But he is right. We pass
safely under the churning bellies of hail clouds.
Twenty miles later we hit clear sky.
In our rearview mirror, we see clouds stacked
so thick it's a miracle they didn't flatten us.

IV

From my sister's home at the edge of town we can see
that whole storm mass stalled over White Rock Colony.
The boys light Lava Cones, exploding paper tanks,
side-winder rockets, and Screaming Bees—delighted
in terror when Atomic Chasers really do chase.

All the while, that black cliff of cloud to the south
pounds lightning in fantastic flashes: purple bolts,
gold hoops, pink webs, blue rivers, green balls that roll
along the horizon and burst into hot white cracks.

Even the boys stop lighting rockets to watch.
We sigh, "Oooh," and "Ahh,"
and "Did you see that one?"

How can that place of deadwood and papery old houses
take being pounded again and again with those bolts?
We tease the boys, say that the lightning might be attracted
to the white gravel they collected in that ghost town.

The sound of that thunder can't travel this far,
yet it seems to shake the trailer. The clear sky whips
with wind so fast, it sounds like flags snapping—
The boys slip inside to hide.

V

I did not mean to trick them, or you,
into thinking that place was cursed.
But, watching the sky, we begin to believe in lightning
on a lonesome search for the long-blasted
white rock and people who belong to that earth.

II
Mysteries of Faith

The Pond

Baltimore's flowers go off like fireworks.
Azaleas buzz in colors too hot for our eyes.
You take me to a pond with a cooling fountain,
a bronze child leaping across lilypads. I'm amazed
when you stamp your feet and the Koi rise to be fed.
We have come to release an overgrown fantail goldfish.
She slips from the plastic bag, glimmers above dull coins,
disappears into waters as filled with wishes as marriage.
I press a penny to my lips, toss it in the depths.

Catch and release, catch and release—we have loved
this way for years. That day at the pond repeats,
it seems. The splashing child never
ages, our reflections always waver. And you
keep stamping at the edge of that pond until
hundreds of fish churn at its surface,
bubbling up with wishes at their lips,
all the best, all for you.

Vegetarian

To "forswear things of the flesh" I thought meant
those spring Fridays we ate no fowl, no meat

or Monday, Wednesday, Thursday during Lent
kneeling at the plaster Stations of the Cross:

from Christ scourged to the temple curtain rent
and the final commendation of the thunderclap.

Jesus, strained marble pale, stumbled or bent
to the splintered Cross, ragged, bloody, all body,

all flesh—my tiny heart billowed like a tent.
No wonder I began to poke and pick at dinner.

By Easter the lily's glimmer convinced me to repent.
Carnivorous in compassion, my brother ate my portion.

Fat in America

This is no joke. She is fat and happy in the U.S.A. The kind of woman who always has plenty of loving men—not just perverts either. You are thinking that she can't be all that fat. Well, she is. There are folds of flesh at the back of her neck—her half-moon cheeks swallow her eyes—her eyes are olives sunk in whole wheat dough—her chin doubles when she laughs, and wobbles when she talks—her shoulders are broad and solid as an XXL man's. Her breasts are vast. There is no other way to say it. Unless we say they are globes of warmth or that she would nurse nations. Oh, she has held a lover's head between them and covered all but his bald spot. And yet she has a waist, still obviously indented beneath a rich ring of belly—her hips rise biblically (mounds, doves, wheat, hills) nothing is fertile enough to describe them, except the Great Plains where she was born. Yes, her hips are like cropland. And the valley between? A gorgeous secret place, a gorge of ferns and falls—her thighs are sacks of grain, a harvest—her calves carved timbers, marble sculpture. And her feet? Ah! These are the platforms of faith—holy and round and strong.

The Execution of Mr. Carp

Carp were garbage eaters,
polluters of the perch pond, criminal,
subject to the full extent of our law.

My brother made me judge. He'd execute
the sentence I learned to repeat:
"Mr. Carp, you are guilty to death."

Condemned, head on the picnic bench edge, the fish
received my last blessing while the executioner
steadied another bench, poised to drop, a guillotine.

This was the shape of childish power
and pity: we sometimes stayed the execution
or played the grieving family. I study that distant

childhood through some sluggish atmosphere.
Only that stunned carp eye rises clearly;
something in the pale bluing lens—

I see how fish, drawn through their sky to ours,
reeled in all unwilling, finally choose:
some flex and fight, some relax as if they've

discovered there *had* been truth all along—
how each of their days pointed to that moment,
how we must be always compelled, traveling

unaware, for suddenly and surely we recognize
the depth and weight of peace as it descends.

That Green Night

"THE NEXT EVENING THEY SLEPT UNDER THE STARS AGAIN.
THIS TIME THOSE TWO FELLOWS CAME AND TOOK THEM UP TO
THEIR HUT ABOVE THE CLOUDS."

STAR HUSBAND STORY, TOLD BY JULIA BADGER IN 1944

Even now, she could give him
a look that would shake him
make him roll *rrrs* through his teeth
like her wolf-mate, sitting there
in his leather office chair,
his awards breathless under glass,
his desk pressed to the wall.

When she thinks of how she loved him—
foolish, she knows, to thank him,
years after all the sparky hot stuff
that drove them down a river road hung
with long-limbed painter's trees.

Did he know how, around that fire,
singing Indian songs, her cheek pressed
to the words humming in his throat,
his arm low on her back—Did he know
how she gave up faith in everything
but the green night around them—
floating against him, his blanket edge
tight around them both, her feet barely
skimming the grass, swaying for hours
until the sky stepped down, opened its bright arms—
Did he know how many years that one night held her?
If he had let go any sooner she would have flown
                              beyond earth with those stars.

Tree That's Gone

Not even a stump left
where that fir stood—
where you ran dumb drunk,
your knot of grief unbound
though all week you had tied it
so tightly it set your mouth in a line,
narrowed your eyes to black curves,
yanked your head straight in its secret.
Drink cut it loose:
you stumbled, hollering to the air
in words so far from their tribe,
no one could translate—
wails that cracked the cold night,
made the stars split the sky.

Little Woman,
I'll never speak your words,
but I understand and understand
the sorrow you cried into that tree.
It's gone now, died of your pain,
your tears drained into the ground.
The tree tapped their hot waters,
drank so deeply it shook,
sighed its lowest branches open
like a woman lifting her skirts,
to reveal you lying there, chin to knees,
gasping like a thing newborn.

Flickers

Abandoned town on the border, I wait
in tedious drilling noise. Flickers,
my sister birds, try a hole. Grub-full
and greedy, they ignore me. Fine, I say,
just fine. When have those birds ever

waited for me? What's in that hole for me?
It is hot while I stalk Flickers for feathers—
red and yellow shafts I mean to collect
for prayer fans. Hen-bodied, they would plummet

so easily. It's a pity they act so disappointed in love.
They make their mates sob sad wet notes that move
them to nest in dead wood. I watch, my gaze still, hot.

Ah! Their wings burn right past me.
One eyes me: the sun in a crushing black rock.
She blots me bone dry, sends me dreaming
through a red and yellow thirst—
this prayer they will teach me.

Sweet Short

If your sweetheart sleeps deeply,
here's a charm for morning:
Keep it dry as sand in your room.
Don't drink at bedtime. Dream of water.
Let yourself wake from the power
of your thirst. No one wants to be alarmed
awake, and this is as good as a clock, even better.

When you wake, pour all you can tell of your dreams
down into the pool of your sweetheart's sleeping ear.
Let the details trickle from your dry lips
into the depths of the sleeper's own dream.
Soon enough you will feel the sleeper rise, like a net
full of catch, like a bucket drawn up a well.

Sex in the Desert

LAS CRUCES, NEW MEXICO

My brain won't admit the desert at first—won't comprehend
heat like a seizure. *Empty* seems too potent a word

for weeks of cloudless unmerciful sky—
Finally, a storm strides toward these Pipe Organ Mountains;

its first drops, big as quarters, sting my skin,
then comes a scent: burned sugar, burning spice—

My blood goes crazy for the sound of wet on dry.
I huff, I snort, I run around the courtyard yelling,

hey, hey, it's raining! My breath comes in deep and high.
Little bugs crawl from every crack in the earth—

The desert is creaking open, spreading herself for love.
Her richness rises in clouds of dust kicked up by rain,

her smell is burned sugar, butterscotch, cinnamon on fire.
The scene's embarrassing, primal: Earth ravaged by Father Sky.

Leaves beat back the rain with a noise like frantic birds;
violent showers send me under a tree bent by water.

The cuckoos and grackles in the branches hoot in a frenzy,
groaning and chortling, letting out manic, sexual cries—

Then it is over. The desert has had enough already.
She just reclines, all wet, delicately steaming as she dries.

Father Sky shags off, withdraws over the desolate mountains.
The cuckoos rise to the bush tops, let out a collective sigh.

Hopi Prophet Chooses a Pop

The light and air? They are mountain-perfect, here in Taos, near
some tennis courts, our conference room door open, all that clear
sun whisking in while we carry on our hot debate in a think-tank of
artists and healers.

We are out to save the world.

My own insomniac clarity lets me see how powerfully ordinary he is,
that Hopi elder, who says humbly, simply, what we somehow knew
was true all along. How sweet his words, clear water rushing cold to
our lips, all the drink we'd ever need—

Until coffee break.

The foam cups lined up, the donuts piled like a stack of spare tires—
I go outside and find him there, nothing between us but bright air
and a tonal vending machine.

That junk's not for me, he says, glancing back to the foyer door, now
blocked by three stainless coffee urns.

No, I reply.

He pats his pockets for glasses. The vending machine sighs.
We approach it respectfully, as teens do juke boxes, as gamblers
do slots.

Read me what she's got, he squints through yellowed lenses. I will admit
it: I hope to divine what he'd like, that my right choice will somehow
reflect how much of his teaching I get—*There's sparkling water*, I try,
jingling my change.

No response but a slight, expectant shift.

There's apple juice, veggie cocktail? I ask, thinking he'd like something
natural. Or *Bubble Up, ginger ale, cream soda*?

I am on a roll call of beverages: *root beer, Crush, Nehi*? As if that
machine contains all the liquids ever canned by human hands,

I list tonic, sarsaparilla, lemon-lime, Coco-yahoo soda, diet this, caffeine-free that,
and all your regular colas.

I appeal to the horizon, source of inspiration, and make one last
certain offer: *Mountain Dew.*
A pause, but no, no response.

Finally I feed in dimes. The coin slot gulps, my own favorite choice
rolls down. Just then the button flashes—machine's all out—And
then, of course, he cries: *That's right! That's right! That one* I *like.*
I'll take that Doctor Pop.

Wearing Indian Jewelry

I was wondering why that guy
wore the blanket coat, bone choker, rock
watch, woven buckle, quilled Stetson—
I was wondering why he wore
that beaded vest, like a ledger drawing
or a Winter Count, its skinny figure
forever sneaking after two bison
around belly to back,
around back to belly—
I was wondering why, when he said,
I *wear these getups every day*—
Every day, because these things
are sacred, these things are prayer.

Then I knew I could live this life
if I had blue horses
painted around and around me,
shells and beads like rain in my ear
praying *Prairie open in me*
at stoplight, hard city, last call, bank line,
coffee break, shopping cart, keycode,
Prairie open in me
Prairie open in me
every day every day every day.

Turtle Rattle

FOR VAL

That prayer shaker hanging there, I've never rattled.
A gift from Billy, up from Oklahoma, I was flattered.
But to shake it, I should make a song I can't yet grasp
about its plates, like moons, a calendar of the past,
a year we would erase, since our friend lost her battle,
sunk dark in Alaska, where she drank a death so hard—
hard to stop the picture, yet we will not say the word,
at least not until our songs can make it matter.
Then we will chant, count years, and raise the rattle.

Ants died working hard to clean flesh from inside
this turtle. Those little sisters now make a part
of the noise—dried ants and small stones scatter
when I shift the shell. I would shake it so hard,
hard for me to pick it up though, to shake, shake.
Stones fall through me, break into ants, shatter.
Rhythm hits us hardest, makes us sadder.
Easier to shy away in rhyme and prattle, prattle.

Sing the truth. Shake a prayer with turtle, turtle
whose endurance at its root means hard, hard.
We are stone, we go on, our two hands lift the rattle.

Earthswimmer

Her good black earth is what draws them. Year after year she takes their dead to cradle, but they tell her nothing. The dead do not talk in their sleep, only mutter and toss, blue in cold caves of dreams.

She has no arms to reach out, so struggles to embrace them with rivers. They pound, dance, wail, stamp for her attention—but live too quickly to hear her stone slow words.

All their tears of grief or greed or laughter are never enough for her. Hasn't she given her back to be raked, risen where they wanted her in mounds? Her heart is stone flame, her tongue molten, a love that could lick us from our mother forever.

Do not expect her to be soft or comprehending. She can dry this land to explosions of dust. The events of our generations mean nothing to her, unless we convey our history. So go on, now. Try to tell her. Only, speak slowly as all time gone by.

Phosphorescence

At the end of love, disaster
sucks all the air from the room,
swings shut doors in our brains' corridors,
hums down like power failure,
switches our skin off.

At the end of love we find a Quaker island
where surf by night breaks glowing
with foam. Tiny creatures whose bodies
make their own light fill the water.
We two strangers wade to the shore,
our own forms lit by the moon.
We wash ourselves of our old, other lives.

Then the crushed-shell beach-path
confuses itself with the horizon of large
white stars hanging so close to the island.
At the end of love, we lose
our balance in a globe of glowing points.

When we reach to steady each other,
low clouds begin to trail above us
in shapes of peaceful spirits.

Wheat Ears

Driving into blue January cold, I take
the short road from the interstate.
Wheat Ears blow like pepper
and salt specks, such tiny birds,
strays from the Alaskan Barrens.
Most migrate to Africa, yet inexplicably,
dozens spend the winter here
along this frozen prairie ditch
miles away from the flat river
that tugs these hills into valley.

Clear purple shadows of snow cast up,
reflect on sheer clouds, color the late day
against an edge of startling green sky
—a color that belongs to this place alone.

Coming into distance, space opens in me
like surprise, expands an eye
grown used to the city's short view—
the sloped lawns and park ponds
with stocked trout, stalked by herons,
as far from North Dakota winter as Africa.

Wheat Ears stand in the road, wait,
wait, then scatter ahead of my wheels,
whirl recklessly near my windshield,
then, like a crowd, resolve in the rear view.

I aim for the end of the highway where
the vivid horizon makes a lid for the sleepy
sun, the red and satisfied eye that God
will close on my home town tonight.

III

Systems of Divination

Translation

Enter the simple landscape
of snow on broken fields,
trust those lines it gives up:
two narrow trees, a dip in the land,
a farmhouse heaved into itself, abandoned.
We go to the doorway, no further—
beyond the threshold we would step into air.
The floor, collapsed as if a bomb dropped,
framed by walls hung with ghostly
impressions of pictures long gone,
tells of a great force. We imagine
that a tornado, noisy as a pressure cooker
caught in the chimney, brought the floor down.
No one home to open east windows,
front door, storm doors to the cellar.
This is a place forever falling on itself,
a story we should recognize.
But we turn in that doorway, face
the blue glare, the horizon flat out like a lover
pressing close to field, rails, road.
We stare until the train tracks
trick our eyes, collide at the edge of sight.
We should go to them, lie side to side,
our ears to the rails, hear the low singing,
smell iron become a flat yet bitter taste.
And if we lie there until the train
makes an eye of light in the sky,
and if we stand or stumble
while the train spins the ground away,
if we watch until we are certain
there is no meeting of those tracks,
would we still think we could break
the law of a land with parallels so vast?
As if we are stories mere touch can translate.

Candy Apple Red

A boy in a shark-finned car
painted sleek-red as candied apples
picks her up for a cruise in the country.
They park on a field road by train tracks.
His sweet talk wraps her like blankets.

The kisses and the straining bone to bone
bring her to the still moment she loves
when the wind steps up to toss
the fragrant leaves of the Russian Olives,
and the green wheat begins to seethe,
breaking wave upon wave into a ditch
glutted with wild rose.

She shuts her eyes, a small girl again,
stretching flat on chill earth to let
the hint of winter bite in her nose.
Each time the boy's mouth closes hers
that girl in her blood begins to sing.

He drops her off five blocks from home.
Long shadows of cottonwood trees
lay bars along her street. As she moves
they fall on her, each a stroke, dark
then bright, a pattern of wheels and spokes.

Then the sun spreading low asks:
Isn't the sky your opal—
laid out, burning, just for you?

Fear and Comfort

In the land my dreams inhabit, three dogs
doze in a heap. Just as I give over to sleep,
one stirs as if I've whistled him home.
He shrugs off the blanket of paws and tails,
rakes the ground with long black nails,
and thrusts his muzzle out to smell my dreams.
Dimly I recollect, he and I first met in a bedtime
tale read by my mother. The monster voice she used
thrilled me. The scarier the better—any excuse
to keep her beside me, so I could to cling to her body.
There were three storybook dog brothers: one has eyes
as big as teacups, the oldest's, eyes big as plates.
It's the saucer-eyed, human-headed, middle brute
who draws toward me tonight. I lie mute,
unbreathing, though I'm no child and I know
fear of darkness equals fear of the unknown.
Yet certainly I sense someone comes closer, closer.
The night absorbs and loosens things horribly—
A face floats free, scares me stone still while it hovers.
For a moment, the features coalesce into my mother's,
then I shift and recognize my own image in the mirror.

I cannot recall how my mother hushed me when I cried,
but trust the lesson of her comfort somewhere inside me.
I hold my hand, trace the lines that etch both our palms.
Whether what's past or to come is told, we cannot know—
written there in language only the body reads.

Le Main de Dieu

Leaving Rodin's garden, we stole
late roses whose loose petals
flew in wind up from the river.
We didn't yet know we were wrong
to tell each other our love was our country
and all the waters of the world
flowed straight to our home.
Who could blame us?—young, in Paris.
Later we woke in covers dusted
with frost, grains of ice still
filtering through our cracked skylight.
We were Rodin's sculpted couple—
pale in that pale city, cupped embracing
in the divine approving palm.
Who could they have been if not us?
Two people innocent with trust—
rocked there, believing, in the hand of God.

Short Hand

"A FLEXIBLE THUMB INDICATES GENEROSITY IN LOVE."
ANONYMOUS PALMIST

For years Grandma's gloves lay
balled up in my top drawer,
a difficult inheritance
I hadn't dared wear.

Pearl buttoned white for Sundays,
navy funeral gloves,
long black ones for dates
to the supper club.

Grandma's taste for the occult
thrilled me. She read the cards,
planted her garden by the stars—
from her I learned that any passing cat
might be shorthand for the future.

She would want to read this book
that unnerves me, about sexual palmistry.
How naked hands look now I've read it—
See the nun with *murderer's thumbs*.
Your dentist's *knotty* hands
could mean disaster.
And my own broad palm?
That means something truly obscene.

We should wear mittens, really,
or gloves, like my Grandmother's
which turn out to be too small for me.
They strain at the wrists, make my thumb stiff
but they relax after some time—
                    That's when I feel her hand in mine.

55

The Wishing Fish

ELIZABETH BISHOP MIGHT HAVE THOUGHT RAINBOW, RAINBOW,
RAINBOW, BUT SHE DID NOT LET THE FISH GO.

In the old, old story the wishing ring
brings joy, then misery, then nothing
but an uneasy lesson of greed and giving.

The Magic Walleye also has a tale:
How he first transforms the angler's
camper into a cottage.

The next wish, for power, drives the fish
into an inky blue fit. It's the waste he hates.
The last precious wish always a plea

to undo earlier wishes. And yet this zero-total
magic sometimes teaches contentment.
The angler sleeps safely in his dry pup-tent.

Hearing these stories, my child-mind whirred—
*If only I had caught that fish,
I'd ask for my own magic first,*

or three more wishes before I let him off the hook.
But none of these solutions could forestall
the fateful progression from joy to dispossession.

I vowed I wouldn't make any wish at all.
Yet, how handsome the fish turned out to be, how tragic.
I underestimated the nature of his enchantment—

his own story more tender than the one we tell:
*Gazing through the translucent globe of the lake, humanity
floats speck-like on the surface, tiny, remote, my own.*

I removed the hook with a pliers, meaning to apologize,
then toss him back. But that's not how it goes.
Three wishes are like something you own.

You guess which I chose:
Money, power, clothes
or peace and freedom for us both?

A Sister for My Father

I try to imagine a sister for my father.
A girl who grew up in a house of men and boys,
who knotted her things in a tablecloth
printed with maple leaves red as her hair,
let slam the screen door, for the last time,
stepped into the blue evening air. No one
hears from her, then thirty years later,
there's her name in an Iowa phone book.
Imagine how I pause at her road:
her house stands against the wind,
weathered silver, in unmown grass,
foxtails hissing along the walk.
Her screen door sighs open,
and by the high northern light
of her kitchen window, I see her bent
over a white kitchen sink. Her fingers,
as tapered as my father's, pare an apple
his same way. She is as thin as he is, her hair
blunt cut, gray as ash. The back of her dress
leaps with a print of fish urgent for water.
When she turns she will show me
what I want in this imagining,
what I've seen ripple through the surface
of my face and my sister's—
the female of my father's face.
I wait to catch her attention
but she will not turn.
I stand and stare until the print
straining up her dress seems to swim.
I try to imagine her over and over,
but she is turned forever from me,
in a kitchen with northern exposure
her back bent at the sink, her knife
poised on the fruit.

Dragging the River

Behind the hospital where we were born, we start across the plank bridge. My sister steps ahead, then stops. Below, the sheriff's department divers drag the cloudy waters. We worry that a child might be lost, then remember the news—the search for a gun that could become a murder weapon.

The morning radio reported this unlikely shooting, shocked everyone with details. Yet no crowd converges where we find ourselves by accident, curiously observing the rubber rafts, grappling lines, and underwater camera equipment.

The water barely moves, only the diver's tank sends up rolling bubbles and puffs of silt that break yellow on the surface. The bottom is clay, we know, we waded across this dangerous spot long ago. The river let us pass.

Below us, the silent divers, in heavy, helmeted suits, move slowly, but still rile the sediment that makes this river thicken up each summer. We watch quietly, each dragging up memories of long days spent on this water.

Bored in our small town, we couldn't resist the river—the tangled bank, not meant for climbing, we clung to until we reached the low spot where deer drank upriver. Or we'd go to spy on lovers parked on the Minnesota side. We watched for both, but came away with only hoof prints, beer cans.

Those slow waters hardly made a noise and yet they promised something. Now even the divers wade away empty-handed. They find no weapon. Later, we hear the wounded victim survives.

Animoosh

A girl surrounded by brothers
has to have a dream. Mine
was to live deep in green woods
near a stream with a dog to protect me.
Not the family dog, that pile of lint
who licked and begged, but some dream
dog who would mysteriously appear.
Heroic canine—swift as a Greyhound,
she'd share her kill. Her markings
would be expressive as a Shepherd's,
mobile brows and a smiling muzzle.
She'd be velvet-pelted as a Bulldog
and as big-jawed to pull me from sink holes,
mud slides. I'd call the mutt Annie,
and when we rested on the cold earth,
breathing the same raw-rabbit breath,
far from home, darkness creaking about us,
Annie's ears twitching, tail swishing—
we could howl all our loneliness into the world.

I was sure that dog would come from my dream.
With my back to the shadow edge of the shelter belt,
I would stare until I saw her—always just beyond me,
bounding through the long field of goldenrod and sun.

*Animoosh is Ojibway for *dog*.

The Cure

TO ANNE ON NANTUCKET

When the humpback's fluke
unfurled to kiss the waves
a place in me once stilled,
tugged with sudden motion.
Surely as landing a kite
I brought my heart back home.

Let the mountain's thin-voiced aspens
go gold in glory of themselves,
pride is nothing against the sea.
Last night a small plane down traceless,
a shrimp boat torn to litter in the surf.
She takes what she wants.

She's a dreaming woman
rocking this island like a lover,
running her tongue along the shore.
Who could resist her? Who wouldn't submit
to the arms and the lips of the sea?

TV News: *Detox Closed*

No comment, just image after image
of the front line troops
in the Alcohol and Indian War—
The camera gives us back a day
with a band of merry tribal drunks
who, by midnight, will wind up
in ER, getting tested and typed,
paying in blood for a night's stay.

On a red carpeted stairway,
a TV newsman stands,
a polished bastard of a banister
glides thirty feet of wood
under his hand. He gazes
from the tube, ironic, amused,
saying that since Detox closed
taxpayers spend $300 per inebriate
on nightly emergency treatment.

He gestures meaningfully
at the parquet floor;
the chandelier winks
at his sick little joke
about the nightly rate
of a honeymoon suite,
which somehow explains
why he's reporting on Detox
from the foyer of a luxury hotel.

Yeah, I'd like to see those guys
put up for a night in the Ritz.
What a party! Sneak in some friends,
by the end of the night we'd drop

the taxpayers' cost to, say,
thirty dollars a head.

More video images, more faces.
I peer at them as through water,
wondering who they were on land.
Street Chiefs, I've heard them called,
a name whose honor is earned backward,
unspoken by the time it's deserved.
Heroes do return, yes, healed like warriors,
but these on TV are still so far away.

There is a battle in a distant country
where breath and drink are twins.
Each swallow, you pull toward that world
whose element is alcohol, not air.
Tilt the bottle to see the entrance,
a hole at the top of the sky, bright as sun,
the glass lip a tunnel toward that land
whose voice always provokes you
come on, come on,
where you belong—

Now tell me you wouldn't go.

The Widow's Grove

Drinking sleep I grow old—
on and on I push through the grove
to a declining orchard
still putting out pale buds.
Trees step into rows.
Faces flicker in the boughs,
familiar, dear, those long gone.
Just when one seems in reach
it's the tree's white sprays
I find in my arms, unfolding
against me, tight with hard pushes
that have not forgotten desire.
When I turn to the marsh
they branch out after me,
but they are not my husband who,
when loving was not enough,
gathered me, sinking, from sleep.

The Quiet Earth

Snow fills the leaves that haven't blown,
inverted umbrellas, they weigh trees down.
The tall elm leans almost into Helen's garden.
Out in her backyard, the winesap branches harden
in an icy armor that will snap those limbs.
In her barn, the auction goes on. Winter comes
too early, freezes the grass and blows away the birds,
blows faintly in the kitchen, in the attic overhead.
Helen's plates, white as eggs, tremble in a stack.
They say ghosts grow loud in hunger and must be fed,
but today she is silent when I want one word back,
an ordinary phrase or the way she shaped my name.

Snow turns to rain. Pools gather on the frozen ground.
The earth's so hard there's nothing it takes in.
Branches crack like lightning strikes: Helen's apple trees.
To her forgotten orchard of windfalls and blight,
we drove on dry dirt roads in the long light
of my childhood summer afternoons.
In exchange for seedlings, my father would prune
or graft a row of trees back into shape.
This was a lonely place, but loud with wind
and overgrown with a kind of ivy, a wild grape
that twined into the trees, tore them to the ground.

I've fixed Helen there forever, so old and light she shook,
her skin like powder and in her eyes a hard blue look—
With my forehead fit into the cup of my palms
I sit for hours, think of apples, think of Helen.
The wind rails, knocks leaves off the elm
whose bare arms hang sad as a willow leaning low.
I press my cheek along the crook of my elbow.
Snow turns to rain. Pools gather on the frozen ground.
The earth's so hard there's nothing it takes in.
Helen's plates, white as eggs, tremble in a stack.
The earth's so hard, there's nothing it gives back.

The Drunk's Spirit

Say a word against that ghost
before you rock off into dreams.
Hope he won't disturb this house
with his stagger and his mean
curse that, when he lived, caused
dishes to dance up and crack,
made lamps pop when he smacked
his fists or boots into the wall.
So ward him off, say the worst:
we don't want him here at all,
don't want to wake to his loud thirst
that broke figurines, toy trains, china cups.
Now all those shards wake us up—
A composition of fragments and rage,
a rattling beast made all of damage.

Born in November

Season of evenings always gray and backlit
by white sun resigning behind terrible clouds
that carry the true snow, the hard snow
of winter begun by Thanksgiving on the Plains.
Imagine being born under such an ominous sky,
just after the assassination—Born into the national
mourning and the wrenching, particular mourning
of young Catholic mothers. Neighbors thought
the shock might have brought on the labor.
And the child will always sense this surrender
—the oblique light, the brown field stubble,
hiss of wind, stars splitting the sky—
She will always love November.

The Visible Woman

was her name—
that plastic model of anatomy,
who wanted to be cousin to dolls.
Her larger size, and lashless eyeballs
washed over by a face sheer as a wave,
her viewable puzzle of lifelike entrails
encased in a skin clear of texture and detail,
terrorized Barbie, even Ken.
Alien, indiscreet, her vitals all too obvious,
she was unwelcome, fled from when she called.
Building block doorways fell as she entered.
Mute, stiff, indelicate, she lacked Barbie's
parting lips, swivel hips and discreet, polished nails.
Her hands, fused into fingerless, scallop-edged cups
on stiff arms held waist-high, palms up,
offered an awful embrace of kinship.

Do you see how any day your inside might out?
You expect to ripen to that blonde plastic body,
while already your skin pures, lifting like a mist,
rinsing free to your most visible core
where blue and red branches, artery and vein,
etch surely to your heart, from your heart, and open-armed,
thumb-pinkie-index-fore meld to raise you like wings.

Future Debris

"THE TYPICAL OBJECT UP THERE IS ABOUT THE SIZE OF
A FILING CABINET."

FROM "SPACE JUNK A DANGER TO LAUNCHES,"
JOHNS HOPKINS GAZETTE, AUGUST 23, 1988

Until he died we thought our neighbor dull.
Now he's a distant point of light.
His cremated body orbits low
in its reflectorized canister creating
what the space burial firm called
"a twinkling reminder of the loved one."
There's a wheel chart to map his course.
Nights we go around back of the house,
gaze at what little true sky winks
through the haze of debris.
It amazes me and is a relief, really,
not to have the whole universe
smack up against me like a wall.
All my life I've strained to comprehend
planets and motion, all the unending
that's been clouded, obscured
by the detritus humans seem to produce
naturally, ink to the squid, protective
cloak through which we cannot see
and therefore feel we are not seen.
Some night, a little girl, who will know
only tame animals, city trees, will listen
to my tales of wilderness and game.
I'll hold her up so she basks in the glint
of celestial jetsam. She will spread her hands,
reach for the bright flecks, ask if they are wild.
Lying to the child, I'll say they are. Then the filing
cabinets, ah, they'll glimmer like stars!

Sense

Streetlights blur, elongated
on the wet reflective pavement.
Under one umbrella, two people
guided by white canes, catch
the rush of a traffic wave, splash
across to the gutter, and are safe.

At the market a deaf couple
sign as they shop the aisles.
They turn from each other, unaware,
and in a moment find their fingers
telling words to air. The man laughs,
thrusts his still-speaking hands into her hair.

Here, now, darkness wraps our bodies.
We float silent, lightless, except where
a slat broken in the blind plays
light across your chest, my neck.
The heat that rises from our skin
gives us voice and vision. You trace
a curve and dot along the plane of my cheek.
My mouth against your collarbone moves
an answer to your question mark: yes, yes.

Heid E. Erdrich

Heid E. Erdrich grew up in Wahpeton, North Dakota, where her parents taught at the Bureau of Indian Affairs Boarding School. She is Metis/Ojibway from Turtle Mountain on her mother's side and German-American on her father's side. Her degrees are from Dartmouth College and Johns Hopkins University. She has worked as a seamstress, cleaning lady, court-scene reporter, teen counselor, police dispatcher, jail matron, bartender, teacher, and multicultural student counselor. Her poetry has been published in anthologies and journals such as *Maryland Poetry Review, Raven Chronicles, Tamaqua, Prairie Volcano*, and others. In 1992, she moved to Minnesota and now teaches English and writing at the University of St. Thomas.

Of her first book collection, she writes, "*Fishing for Myth* shows the creation of personal myth. When events or memories seem impossible or inexplicable, I listen for the voice that tells how they came to be—the story voice, the myth-teller. These poems are the result of that listening."

5824